CW01271004

Copyright © 2023 by Ken Cunliffe
www.detectorist.com / www.detectorists.com

Beneath Our Feet - volume 2
First Printing, 2023

All rights reserved. No part of this publication may be reproduced, distributed, or transmitted in any form or by any means, including photocopying, recording, or other electronic or mechanical methods, without prior written permission.

Each detectorist supplied their own photos, bios, and descriptions, which are used with their permission. Wood/sand/beach background images, as well as country flag icons, are licensed stock photography images used within licensing guidelines.

I would like to express my heartfelt gratitude to all the detectorists who have eagerly contributed to this book, as well as volume 1. The wonderful discoveries you've made and the captivating stories you've shared have truly enriched its content. Thank you for being a part of this incredible journey!

All the finds celebrated in this book are "natural" finds. Nothing contained in these pages is from a seeded hunt.

Do you have an amazing find you would like celebrated in a future volume of Beneath Our Feet? If so, send an email to ken@detectorist.com and include a short description of the find along with a photo.

BENEATH OUR FEET
volume 2

KEN CUNLIFFE

RECOVERING LOST HISTORY

DETECTORIST.COM

RECOVERING LOST HISTORY

DETECTORIST.COM

TABLE OF CONTENTS
(alphabetical order by first name)

FOREWORD	10
INTRODUCTION	12
ALISON WALKER	16
ALLYSON COHEN	18
AMANDA DEGAZ	20
AMBER CARTE	22
ANDREI ROTAR	24
ANDY SNELL	26
BRANDON NICHOLAS	28
BRIAN D'AUST	30
BRIAN OUHRABKA	32
BRIAN YERDON	34
CARMEN RITTER	36
CAROL RIO	38
CHIP KIRKPATRICK	40
CODY DRAKE	42
CORIELTAVI LISA	44
DANIEL GHERASIM	46
DANIEL MOSS	48

DAVE SADLER	50
DWIGHT COLON	52
FRANK LOPERGOLO	54
FRANK NEAL	56
HEATH JONES	58
JAMES OPFAR	60
JASON JONES	62
JEDIDIAH CARROLL	64
JEFF LUBBERT	66
JIM CHARUHAS	68
JOANNE SHEPHEARD	70
JOHN M BRADBURY	72
JOHN MacEACHEN	74
JOHN PORCELLA	76
KEVIN RUDD	78
KURT FRANZ	80
LAURIE GAGNE	82
LEIGHTON HARRINGTON	84
LISA JONES	86

TABLE OF CONTENTS
(continued)

MARCUS READ	88
MATT HOWELL	90
MATTHEW PEARCE	92
MICHAEL BISSONNETTE	94
NATHAN DINNING	96
PAUL PRICE-TUPPER	98
PHIL MYERS	100
ROB HILT	102
ROBERT JOHNSON	104
SID PERRY	106
STEF TANGUAY	108
STEVE MOORE	110
STEVE WARREN	112
SUE ROBERTS	114
TOM GEER	116
TONY MANTIA	118

FOREWORD

Welcome to Volume Two. The author has assembled another amazing collection of unique and interesting folks, along with their recoveries. Men and women, young and old, diverse individuals from around the world, all share the dream and passion of finding something lost long ago. It's a part of our psyche. It's embedded in our DNA. It's what we think about constantly. We are curious creatures, and we want to know the history behind everything we find. And we delight in sharing that information with anyone who will listen. We detect, we dig, and we get dirty... a lot. But for us, it is absolutely worth the time and effort. For a moment in time, finding something satisfies us, and then it's time to start searching again.

The truth is we are just temporary stewards of everything we find. And everything we find has a story. One day those stories will be lost or forgotten. That's why these books are so important. They capture the essence of each person and the finds they share within these pages. There are so many other folks whose stories deserve to be told, and their finds documented. That's why I am delighted that Ken has assembled another volume. My hope is that this will continue to grow, and over time even more people and recoveries will be documented in future volumes.

Finally, as I did in Volume one, I encourage everyone to read and contemplate Ken's introduction. It paints a wonderful portrait of who we are and why we look for things beneath our feet.

Marc Hoover
Adventures In History

INTRODUCTION

Have you ever wondered what lies beneath the surface of the ground we walk upon? What lost treasures, long-forgotten relics, and stories of the past are waiting to be discovered? The hobby of metal detecting holds the key to unlocking a world of wonders buried beneath our feet. It is a pursuit that connects us to history in a profound and tangible way, weaving a thread through time and allowing detectorists to become time travelers.

In the quiet solitude of early mornings or the golden hues of sunset, detectorists embark on a journey of exploration and curiosity. Armed with their trusty metal detectors, they traverse fields, beaches, forests, and forgotten homes, searching for echoes of the past. With each swing of the coil, a symphony of beeps and chirps, a language only they can decipher, reveals the presence of buried artifacts and lost treasures.

But metal detecting is more than just a hobby—it is a window into the stories and lives of those who walked the same paths we tread today. With every unearthed coin, button, relic, or lost ring, we are transported back in time, connecting with the intricate tapestry of human existence. It is a thrill that stirs the soul and ignites the fervor of detectorists around the world.

Imagine the joy of discovering a Roman coin, an item from a civilization that thrived many centuries ago. Contemplate the weight of history as you hold in your hands an axe head, crafted by an ancient hunter on a quest for survival. Feel the whispers of a bygone era as you unearth a wartime medal, a poignant reminder of the sacrifice and resilience of generations past. These artifacts are not mere trinkets—they are gateways to a world long gone, beckoning us to uncover its secrets.

With each find, we become part of a vast network of individuals connected through the shared wonder of discovery. We pour over historical records, maps, and books, researching and understanding the context of our finds. We gather in local clubs, online forums, and at

INTRODUCTION
(continued)

organized events, exchanging stories, knowledge, and expertise. We are united in our passion for uncovering the past and preserving its memory.

However, metal detecting is not without its challenges and ethical responsibilities. Detectorists understand the importance of responsible digging, leaving no trace behind, and obtaining proper permissions to search on private lands. We recognize the significance of preserving archaeological sites, collaborating with professionals, and reporting significant discoveries to protect our shared heritage.

Within these pages, we celebrate incredible finds unearthed by passionate detectorists around the world, offering a glimpse into the hidden treasures that lie beneath our feet.

Ken Cunliffe
Detectorist.com

ALISON WALKER

Bio: Alison is from Toronto, Ontario, Canada. She hunts with Minelab Manticore, Equinox 800, and Excalibur 2 detectors. Alison has been detecting for more than 13 years and is a registered metal/hookah/scuba detectorist with the global organization "THE RING FINDERS." You can find her on YouTube and Facebook as "Pink Power Ally Treasure Hunter" and on Instagram as "PinkPowerAlly."

Find Info: Mrs. Wilson lost her gold ring more than 30 years ago in the waters of Lake Muskoka. Her daughter has been a friend of mine since high school, and I was invited up to the Wilson cottage to celebrate all of our 60th birthdays. I brought all my gear with me to see if I could find the ring. After more than an hour of searching, I couldn't believe I was able to recover her ring! Mrs. Wilson cried tears of joy and hasn't taken the ring off since!

Mrs. Wilson's Long Lost Gold Ring

ALLYSON COHEN

Bio: Allyson is from Danbury, Connecticut. She has been metal detecting for 15 years and hunts with a Minelab Equinox and E-trac. Allyson's passion for the hobby led her to create the DetectingDiva.com blog, where she writes about metal detecting from a female perspective. Her articles and finds have been featured in American Digger and The Searcher magazines, and she has been the Northeast Field Rep for American Digger magazine for the past four years.

Find Info: My favorite find is an Indian trade silver brooch from the 1700s (also called a Luckenbooth brooch), which I discovered at the site of a Revolutionary War encampment in New York state. This is special to me not only because it is the only one of these I've ever found, but it's also beautiful. The condition is amazing—even after having been buried for over two centuries!

1700s Indian Trade Silver Brooch

AMANDA DEGAZ

Bio: Amanda "Digger" Degaz lives in Maine, and she is currently using the Minelab Equinox 800. She hosts a podcast on Monday nights called 'Treasure Vortex' with co-host Gypsy Jewels. Amanda showcases her finds on YouTube, TikTok, and Instagram under the name @DiggerDegaz.

Find Info: One of my favorite finds is this Atlanta Arsenal-style CSA belt buckle. The excitement of finding this in Maine makes it truly special. I discovered it during my first year of detecting at an old home site where I had permission to detect. We believe it may have been brought back after the Civil War. I found it using a White's MXT detector.

Atlanta Arsenal CSA Belt Buckle

AMBER CARTE

Bio: Amber is from Federal Way, Washington. She hunts with a Minelab Equinox 800 and a Garrett AT Pro. While Amber's primary detecting area is in Washington, she has also had the pleasure of digging in Montana, Oregon, Hawaii, and England. Amber owns and manages Dirt2art, a YouTube channel, as well as an online nostalgia store.

Find Info: This coin was discovered near Seattle, Washington, on an old home site that has now become a park. The park typically yields Wheaties and toy cars, so finding a coin of this age was a significant surprise. Moreover, it was uncovered during the COVID-19 pandemic. Despite my buddy's initial impulse to clean it by spitting on it—yuck!—I still go detecting with him!

Two Cent Piece
1869

ANDREI ROTAR

Bio: Andrei Rotar started metal detecting in 2019 and hunts with the Minelab CTX3030 as well as an Equinox 800. He has traveled to England twice with his uncle to hunt for hammered coins and successfully recovered them on each trip! Andrei is already looking forward to going back to England for a third time in September 2024. He says the UK detecting hype is real!

Find Info: I recovered this 1279 Edward 1st hammered silver penny on my September 2023 Colchester, England metal detecting tour. Obverse – WAR ANGL. Reverse – CIVI/TAS/CAN/TOR – Canterbury mint.

1279 Edward 1st
Hammered Silver Penny

ANDY SNELL

Bio: Andy hails from Spring Grove, Pennsylvania, and has been metal detecting since 2013. He currently uses a Minelab Manticore and an Equinox 900. Over the years, Andy has recovered many unique finds, including 121 Kennedy half dollars in a creek, which can be seen on his YouTube channel "LOST BOYS RECOVERY." Andy enjoys relic and water hunting, camping, and working on motorcycles in his spare time.

Find Info: I recovered this 1923 National Motorcycle Gypsy Tour watch FOB alongside Route 30, not far from my home in PA. This discovery holds immense sentimental value for me, given my extensive background as a motorcycle mechanic spanning over 25 years.

1923 Watch FOB
National Motorcycle Gypsy Tour

BRANDON NICHOLAS

Bio: Brandon (aka Adventure Archaeology) has been a treasure hunter for over 25 years and uses a Garrett ATMAX. Brandon's dad started him young, metal detecting and searching for arrowheads. As time went on, he became an antique bottle digger, which is what has gained him popularity on his Facebook and YouTube channels!

Find Info: The Virginia Militia button pictured was found while searching with the Garrett Field team in North Carolina. Predating the Civil War, this button packs a serious punch when it comes to history! The face depicts the Virginia coat of arms with "Virtus" slaying the Tyrant! It also says "Sic Semper Tyrannis," meaning "thus always to tyrants" in Latin.

Virginia Militia Button
1830s

BRIAN D'AUST

Bio: Brian D'Aust has been metal detecting for more than 6 years and swings the Minelab Equinox 600 and Minelab Manticore. He loves detecting for War of 1812 relics, as it played a major role in his hometown of Plattsburgh, New York. Brian has discovered several camps, including three previously unhunted sites that produced hundreds of buttons and various relics.

Find Info: My favorite find is from the War of 1812, an artificer button. The Corps of Artificers was made up of 129 men and were master craftsmen in many different fields. The button can be found on pages 61-62 of Albert's button book and was of the 26 mm variety with an RV value of 150. It is extremely rare, and I am honored to have saved it.

War of 1812
Artificer Button

BRIAN OUHRABKA

Bio: Brian resides in Alton, New Hampshire, and uses both the Minelab Equinox 800 and the Manticore. He has been metal detecting since 2013 and has made numerous trips to Colchester, England.

Find Info: On my second trip to Colchester, I was on a field that had never been detected before. I was digging everything non-ferrous, as hammered coins can register at extremely low VDI. Suddenly, a small yellow disc emerged from the ground, and I stared at it in utter disbelief. Could it be? My very first gold coin! A Henry IV quarter Noble — a coin from the light coinage minted between 1412 and 1413. Given Henry IV's brief reign, these coins are rare, making it incredibly fortunate that I can now claim it as my most remarkable discovery to date.

1412-13 Henry IV
Gold Quarter Noble

BRIAN YERDON

Bio: Brian resides in Syracuse, NY, and has been metal detecting for more than ten years. He hunts with the Nokta Legend as well as the Minelab Equinox 800. Brian loves the fact that every outing is a new adventure with endless possibilities and a surprise in every hole. He also loves the camaraderie with fellow detectorists!

Find Info: 1910 parade ribbon pin given to attendees (delegates) of a fire convention held in Syracuse, NY. The ribbon, of course, is missing. The car itself is a Franklin, which was only manufactured in Syracuse and only for a short period of time. The automobile motif is to recognize the ongoing motorization of the fire service at that time. The Syracuse Fire Department was motorized by 1912. To the best of my knowledge, this pin is pretty rare, and only a very small handful are known to exist.

1910 Fire Convention Parade Ribbon Pin

CARMEN RITTER

Bio: Carmen Ritter is a resident of East Garafraxa, a small town in Ontario, Canada. He hunts with the XP Deus II and Minelab Manticore. Carmen is passionate about assisting owners of old homes in connecting with the history of their properties. His work involves uncovering relics, artifacts, and coins left by previous family members or owners, which can be both educational and emotional.

Find Info: Silver Denarius. Marcus Aurelius reigned from 161–180 AD. The long, pointed beard and curly hair should make this easily identifiable as Aurelius. This coin dates from December 165 AD through the summer of 166 AD. Recovered in Colchester, England, during my September 2023 hunt.

Marcus Aurelius Silver Denarius 165-166AD

CAROL RIO

Bio: Carol lives in the Hudson Valley, NY area and has been detecting for over 40 years. She currently hunts with the Garrett AT Gold with the NEL 11" Super Fly coil. Carol has always had a love for history and feels a special connection with our past when recovering personal objects. She currently works with local historical societies on their properties and gladly donates her finds back to the museums for future generations to see and enjoy.

Find Info: Inner tongue of a Civil War Wreath buckle inscribed with the initials MCB. I researched this buckle, and it was agreed by Civil War diggers that it is the same style as a band buckle. It could be attributable to the "Marlboro Cornet Band." It is considered quite rare by Civil War collectors.

Civil War Wreath Buckle
"Marlboro Cornet Band"

CHIP KIRKPATRICK

Bio: Chip is from Florida and started metal detecting in 2011. His finds have been published in magazines in the US, England, and Scotland, including the cover of American Digger Magazine twice.

Find Info: While near the NE Florida / SE Georgia border, I recovered this medallion, initially mistaken for a can lid. Closer inspection revealed it as a Scottish silver piece with intricate engravings, including the Gaelic slogan "I Make Sicker" (I Mak Siccar), MY FAMILY'S MOTTO! The medallion's origins arouse curiosity. In 1733, James Oglethorpe formed the Georgia colony, recruiting Highlanders to thwart the northward Spanish expansion from Florida. Their Amelia Island settlement, near my discovery, adds depth to this historical enigma.

Silver Scottish Medallion
1299 Historical Enigma

41

CODY DRAKE

Bio: Cody (aka The Arizona Treasure Hunter) is from Gilbert, Arizona. He has made several television appearances, including the Discovery Channel, Travel Channel, and several documentaries, as an expert on Treasure Hunting and Desert Survival. He has also been featured in magazines and news interviews for Treasure Hunting discoveries. Cody's site is ArizonaTreasureAdventures.com, and his Facebook page is "The Arizona Treasure Hunter."

Find Info: This is an unfired 56-50 Spencer Cartridge, which was made for the 1865 Spencer carbine. This would have been used during the Apache Wars and was found on a permission that was the site of many Apache raids.

1865 Spencer Carbine
56-50 Cartridge

CORIELTAVI LISA

Bio: Corieltavi Lisa (AKA Lisa Grace) has been metal detecting for more than 20 years and is currently using the XP Deus. She hunts all over the UK, as well as in other countries in Europe. Lisa has handed in 18 treasure finds to the British Museum, many of which are gold. She is well known for researching and recovering Celtic coins made of gold, silver, bronze, and potin.

Find Info: I am also well known for the Chew Valley Treasure, which I found with friends in January 2019. The valuation for this hoard is £5-6.5 million, making it the most valuable treasure ever discovered in the UK. The 2,528 coins were from William the Conqueror, Harold II, and Edward the Confessor. I will never forget the feeling of digging into the red mud of the Chew Valley and finding hundreds of very shiny, greatly preserved coins of the highest rarity.

1066-87 William the Conqueror Chew Valley Treasure

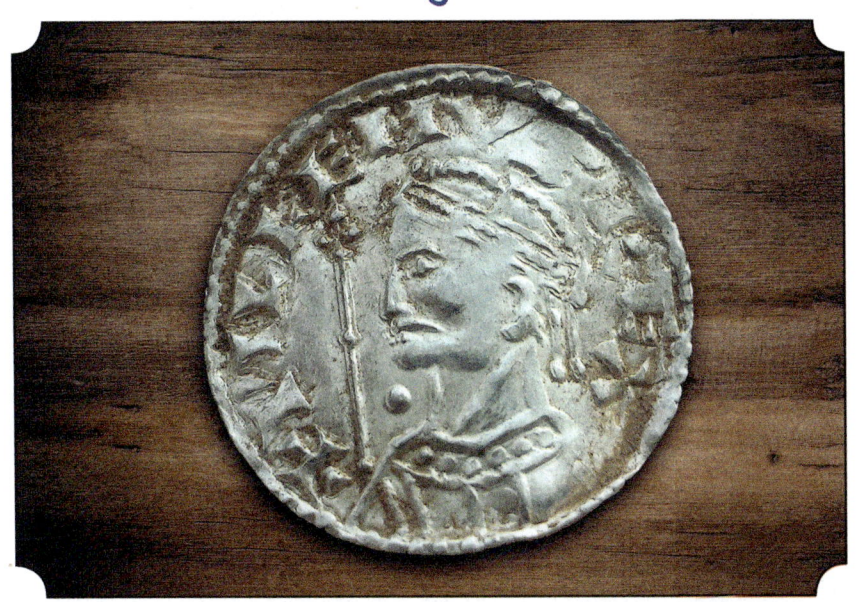

DANIEL GHERASIM

Bio: Daniel lives in Naples, Florida, and his journey into the exciting world of metal detecting began back in 2016 when he got his first detector. Right from the start, he was absolutely hooked on this thrilling hobby. Over the years, he's had the pleasure of metal detecting in numerous places around the world using various metal detectors, including the XP Deus, Minelab Equinox 800, and a Minelab CTX3030.

Find Info: Scotland 1602 James VI hammered silver 8th Thistle Merk, 1 shilling and eight pence (20 pence). Found in Colchester, England, during a September 2023 tour. Obverse - JACOBUS 6 D.G.R SCOTORUM. Reverse - REGEM IOVA PROTEGIT 1602.

Scotland 1602 James VI
8th Thistle Merk

DANIEL MOSS

Bio: Dan Moss is from North Norfolk, England. He uses a Nokta Legend as well as a Minelab Manticore and is part of the Dragon Detecting team. Dan is also known as "Digger Dan" and runs a Facebook group and YouTube channel called "Digger Dan Metal Detecting." Dan is passionate about the hobby and loves the history of the finds we pull up from the soil.

Find Info: My favorite find has to be this 60-35 BC Iceni Tribe, Norfolk Wolf, left type full gold stater. Found on my permission in a field full of Roman history, this coin means a lot to me as it is a symbol of where I grew up and have lived all of my life.

Iceni Tribe Norfolk Wolf Full Gold Stater 65-30BC

DAVE SADLER

Bio: Dave has been detecting since he was 4 years old and uses a Minelab Equinox 800. He founded the Archaeology and Metal Detecting magazine in 2015. This magazine provides everyone with the ability to access newsworthy articles, research documents, and much more. Alongside Co-editor Luke Higgins, the magazine now prints several times a year. In 2018, the original podcast format of the BIG Detecting show aired and evolved during COVID into the longest-running weekly TV stream in the world. The show features guests in the metal detecting industry and other associated historical matters.

Find Info: These trench art pieces were modified from old copper pennies and fashioned into various shapes. This particular piece is in the guise of a Spitfire. To think somebody made this with their own hands makes it my favorite find.

WW2 Trench Art Penny Aeroplane

DWIGHT COLON

Bio: Dwight is from Orlando, Florida, and is 41 years old. He has been metal detecting for more than 17 years and is currently using the Nokta Legend and the Minelab Equinox. Dwight loves the vibe metal detecting offers. He has a passion for history and enjoys recovering awesome relics from the people of the past. You can follow Dwight on Facebook and Instagram under "NEW AGE GOONIES."

Find Info: My favorite find is a vintage 1930-1940s 4-carat wedding ring set. I was at one of my daughter's gymnastics competitions in South Carolina, and I snuck away while my family was having breakfast to detect an old lot that was formerly a plantation.

4-Carat Wedding Ring Set
1930-1940s

FRANK LOPERGOLO

Bio: Frank has been detecting for over 35 years and has been hosting the "DETECT AMERICA" podcast with his buddies for more than a decade. The "UGLY BOX" has been his passion for 30 years, and hopes to continue development for many years to come.

Find Info: "Sailor Boy Tavern" served as the covert headquarters for colonial troops that seized ships entering the Delaware Bay region of New Jersey. At one point, it was commanded by General Benedict Arnold. The site was truly astonishing, making headlines in the Philadelphia area news and yielding a remarkable number of reales. The group photo features my 20 reales found during three days of hunting the site.

1788 Spanish 2 Reales
From The Sailor Boy Tavern Site

FRANK NEAL

Bio: Frank is a longtime resident of Lyme, NH, and is now enjoying retirement in Grayson, GA. He has been gold prospecting and metal detecting since the early 1990s and uses the Minelab CTX3030. Frank is a lifetime member of the L.D.M.A. and a member of B.O.N.E., the Best of the Northeast metal detecting club. Frank has traveled to England to detect more than 30 times.

Find Info: In March of 2018, while detecting in Colchester, England, I recovered this beautiful Roman Emperor Claudius gold coin. It was minted in Lugdunum, now Lyon, France, in 41/42 A.D. The obverse shows the head of Claudius right, and the reverse, Constantia seated left. 19mm, 7.70g.

Roman Emperor Claudius Gold Aureus 41-42 AD

HEATH JONES

Bio: Heath started detecting in 1992. His appearance on the TV show "Gold Trails" in 2015 paved the way for the creation of the "History Seekers" channel on YouTube, which also became a sensation on Facebook. Heath's remarkable discoveries have graced the pages of magazines and newspapers, making him a recognized figure in historical exploration.

Find Info: This distinct artillery projectile, specific to that battle, could have originated from only one of four unique guns — all of which were exclusively issued to Holcomb's Battery, a part of the 2nd Vermont Light Artillery. Its extraordinary preservation is a marvel, especially considering the Confederates' practice of repurposing such misfired rounds during their desperate isolation.

3.67-inch Sawyer Bolt
1863 Siege of Port Hudson

JAMES OPFAR

Bio: James Opfar resides in Mountain Home, Idaho. He started metal detecting in Washington State in 2016 and currently uses the XP Deus. James posts his adventures on Facebook and YouTube under "Tough Run Metal Detecting," and you can visit his website at ToughRunMetalDetecting.com.

Find Info: My oldest find, and one of my most interesting, is this copper daguerreotype photograph of a man in a suit. This type of photograph was invented in 1839 and was phased out by 1860. It was found at my first private permission obtained here after moving, near where the Oregon Trail passes through town.

Copper Daguerreotype Photograph

JASON JONES

Bio: Jason lives in Norfolk, England. He has been detecting for four years, using XP and Minelab detectors, and is part of "Team Regton" based in the UK. Jason is known on YouTube as "The Norfolk Button Boy." You can also find him on Facebook and Instagram as "Norfolk_Button_Boy" and on TikTok under the name "metal_detecting_uk."

Find Info: The design motif may be a representation of the World Tree Yggdrasil, with the great serpent Nidhogg weaving around the tree. The smaller creature could represent the squirrel Ratatosk or one of the other serpents who called Yggdrasil home. The features of the enlaced animals — small heads, oval eyes, the open figure eight, the wide, flat ribbon-like bodies — are typical of the Urnes style. Urnes style decoration was produced between around 1030 and 1100 A.D.

Viking Pressblech Die Urnes Style 1030-1100

JEDIDIAH CARROLL

Bio: Jedidiah is 42 years old and lives in Maple Falls, Washington. He has been metal detecting for more than seven years, using a Minelab Equinox 800, and recently purchased an XP Deus 2. Jedidiah mainly hunts logging camps, CCC camps, old homesites, and curb strips. You can find Jedidiah online under the moniker "Diggingthepnw."

Find Info: I found my 1892 Morgan Silver Dollar with a Carson City mint in the town of Anacortes, Washington. I recovered it at an old home site that had burned down and was then leveled. Numerous other silver coins were found there, as well as an 1898 Anacortes dog tax tag.

1892 Morgan Silver Dollar
Carson City Mint

JEFF LUBBERT

Bio: Jeff started detecting in 1978 and currently hunts with the XP Deus II and the Minelab Manticore. He is currently the president of Eureka! Treasure Hunters Club, based in the Denver, Colorado area. Jeff has been a member of The Ring Finders since 2010 and was selected as Ring Finder of the Year in 2011. Jeff has been the co-host of American Digger magazine's podcast, Relic Roundup, since 2010. He has detected in 28 states, 1 U.S. territory, and 8 foreign countries.

Find Info: My favorite find is a Liberty Head 1857-S $2.50 gold piece that I found at an old military outpost from the 1870s out on the eastern plains of Colorado. I placed it in a bezel and wear it on special occasions!

1857-S Liberty Head $2.50 Gold Piece

JIM CHARUHAS

Bio: Jim Charuhas is from Charlestown, New Hampshire. He started detecting more than 11 years ago with the Garrett AT Pro. Jim currently hunts with a Minelab Equinox 800 and an XP Deus II. You can watch Jim's videos on YouTube under "MontshireDigger."

Find Info: My favorite find is this 1812-21 Artillery Eagle button. Amazingly, there were eight other Artillery Eagle buttons in the same hole, along with six other miscellaneous buttons. All of these buttons were found on a private permission in Fitzwilliam, New Hampshire. I was honored to have shared some of the buttons with the homeowner.

Artillery Eagle Button
1812-1821

JOANNE SHEPHEARD

Bio: Joanne Shepheard lives in March, a town in Cambridgeshire, England, UK. She has always used XP machines and recently upgraded to the new XP Deus II. Joanne has been metal detecting for more than 20 years and posts all of her finds on TikTok under the name 'jammy.jo.'

Find Info: One of my favorite finds is this 14th-century bronze seal matrix, found last year in a field in Norfolk. Likely to have been a canon's ecclesiastical seal, it has a person's head in the center, surrounded by six symbols: a cooking pot, a chalice, an eagle, a cinquefoil, a lion passant, and a hand. All are presumed to indicate certain strengths.

Bronze Seal Matrix
14th-Century

JOHN M BRADBURY

Bio: John is from Lancashire, United Kingdom. He has used many brands of detectors and is currently using the Minelab Manticore, Equinox 900, and the Quest 35. John has been metal detecting for more than 35 years and enjoys the fun he has with his fellow detecting brothers. He hunts pastures, farms, rivers, and beaches, searching for historical artifacts and coins. You can follow John on his YouTube channel, "John's Detecting Adventures."

Find Info: One of my favorite finds is a 4,000-year-old Bronze Age axe head, a votive offering recovered in Lancashire, United Kingdom. It was a pagan belief for people before Christianity to bury a precious symbol for their gods for good luck.

Bronze Age Axe Head Votive Offering

JOHN MacEACHEN

Bio: John lives in Perthshire, Scotland. He has been metal detecting since 2000 and is currently using an XP Deus II. John's YouTube channel is "The Scottish Detectorist," and it has gained more than 33,000 subscribers since 2021. You can also find him on TikTok, Instagram, and Facebook as "VisitScotlandTours," where he has around one million followers as a historian and tour guide. John combines that history and knowledge into his metal detecting channel to bring coins and relics to life!

Find Info: I attended a Detectival Rally held in Gloucestershire in September 2021. Incredibly, the gold coin was on the surface in a clod of soil next to a tin can, apparently having been dug out at the same time as the tin can by another detectorist who failed to re-check the hole!

1377-1399 King Richard II Quarter Gold Noble

JOHN PORCELLA

Bio: John Porcella is originally from Far Rockaway, New York, and currently lives in Jacksonville, Florida. He has been metal detecting since the 1970s and currently hunts with the XP Deus II and the Minelab Manicore.

Find Info: My favorite find is this mid-to-late 1700s anchor. I was metal detecting in Flagler Beach, Florida, when I initially uncovered one of the flukes. It took two hours to uncover fully and created quite a stir in the community. I was credited for the discovery by the Historical Society, and the anchor remains there, buried in the sands of time.

Mid-to-Late 1700s Anchor

KEVIN RUDD

Bio: Kevin is 37 years old and is from Holly Hill, South Carolina. He has been metal detecting for more than 3 years and swings the Nokta Makro Legend. Kevin created a group called "Woodland Metal Detecting," and they document their adventures on YouTube. He enjoys filming their finds for everyone to see and would love to have you tag along with them on their adventures to see the incredible history that they save! Check out "Woodland Metal Detecting" on YouTube!

Find Info: In August 2023, within a little town called Galloway, I made one of my most amazing discoveries to date: a 1786 - 14-J Moris New Jersey State Copper coin. Since the beginning, I made it a personal mission to search and find this incredibly hard-to-find piece of history! And I did!

New Jersey State Copper 1786

KURT FRANZ

Bio: Kurt is from Baltimore, Maryland, and is currently treasure hunting with the Minelab Equinox 800, Nokta Legend, and Garrett AT Max. His passion is finding the coins and relics that our Founding Fathers lost while building this country.

Find Info: In the summer of 2023, we were metal detecting in the water at an early 1600s tobacco port. I uncovered a black silver coin that, at first, I figured was a Spanish 1 Real from its size. I flipped it over to see the bust of Lord Baltimore gleaming back at me. I was immediately in disbelief. This is the coin I've joked about finding my entire life. These coins, in any denomination, are extremely rare. The video of me just about fainting can be seen on YouTube under The Hoover Boys.

1659 Lord Baltimore Hammered Silver 6 Pence

LAURIE GAGNE

Bio: Laurie Gagne (aka Goldie) is the host of the TV show "Red River Gold" and her YouTube channel "Relic Dirtyhands." She has been a treasure hunter her entire life and started metal detecting 15 years ago in her hometown of Quebec, Canada.

Find Info: Believed to have been privately minted around the 1830s, some might consider it a counterfeit, but it wasn't created to resemble an existing coin. It was believed to be made as a mockery of the unpopular Governor of the time. The makers used a bust that resembled a trapper. This way, if caught with these coins, they could claim they were used for trade and not as currency. In the word 'Vexator,' they intentionally designed the X to look like an N. 'Vexator' with an X in Latin means 'Tormentor of Canada,' while 'Venator' with an N means 'Trapper of Canada.' Only about 400 of these coins are known to exist.

1830s Vexator Canadiensis
VC-3A1

LEIGHTON HARRINGTON

Bio: Leighton Harrington is from Cape Cod, Massachusetts. He has been metal detecting for more than 50 years and uses a Minelab CTX 3030 and XCaliber 2. Leighton is a professional treasure hunter, talk show host, and seminar presenter. He has made several significant finds over the years, including a $51,000 diamond ring which he returned to the owner.

Find Info: My favorite find is a 1792 Wax Seal that was authenticated to have been hand-carved by the Philadelphia Engravers that George Washington commissioned for 'The Great Seal' of the USA.

Philadelphia Engravers
1792 Wax Seal

LISA JONES

Bio: Lisa Jones lives in Norfolk, England, and has been metal detecting alongside her husband, Jason Jones (also known as Norfolk Button Boy), for the last 4 years. She uses the XP Deus and is part of Team Regton based in the United Kingdom. Lisa has a YouTube/TikTok channel called 'Norfolk Girl Detects,' as well as Instagram/Facebook accounts called 'Norfolk_girl_detects.' She finally got to do the gold dance twice in 2023! Happy Deus!

Find Info: One of my favorite finds is this beautiful full gold stater, Ambiani Series E Uniface Gallic War Stater struck 58-54 BC.

Uniface Gallic War Stater
Full Gold Stater 58-54BC

MARCUS READ

Bio: Marcus lives in Colchester, England, which was once the ancient Roman Capital, Camulodunum. Detecting since 2020, he swings both the XP Deus II and Minelab Manticore and is part of the LP Metal Detecting team. Marcus is known as "Notched To 11" on his YouTube channel, where he shares his exploits in the fields of Essex, UK.

Find Info: Obverse: diademed head facing right inside a serpent circle. Reverse: cross with annulet on each side with a bird facing right. Found in Cambridgeshire on my friend Tom's field; it was my very first bit of Saxon and one of my best days detecting!

Silver Saxon Sceatta
675 AD

MATT HOWELL

Bio: Matt Howell has been treasure hunting for over 10 years and thoroughly enjoys all aspects of the hobby. In recent years, he has developed a particular passion for hunting with the Minelab GPX series of metal detectors in highly mineralized ground. Matt is also an avid scuba diver.

Find Info: A few years ago, I recovered the ID stencil of James Wolf Bradley, a Civil War soldier who fought with the 2nd New York Cavalry throughout the American Civil War. It is an incredible artifact to hold and to be able to put a name to. It's highly unlikely that I will ever find something so personal again.

Civil War ID Stencil
James Wolf Bradley

MATTHEW PEARCE

Bio: Matthew Pearce is 37 years old and lives in North, South Carolina. He started metal detecting in 2020 and still uses the detector he started out with, a Minelab Equinox 600. He feels blessed to have been able to dig up some great relics in the few years he has been detecting.

Find Info: Only daffodils in the spring and scattered broken pottery revealed that it was once an old homesite. Found 8 inches deep with a bent nail somewhat masking the target, but the Equinox sniffed it out. I believe the house was built in the late 1700s or early 1800s, according to the broken pottery and pewter flat buttons found.

1851 Seated Half Dime

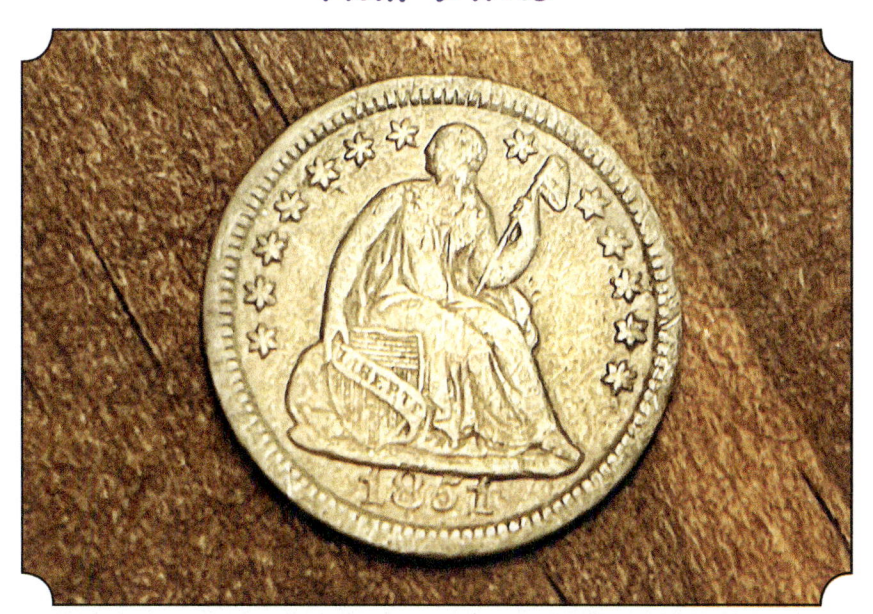

MICHAEL BISSONNETTE

Bio: Michael Bissonnette is from Salem, New Hampshire, and he is currently using a Nokta Legend detector. You can follow him on his website, Digfortreasures.com.

Find Info: I found this extremely rare 53rd Regiment British foot soldier's belt plate in Chester, New Hampshire, on private permission using my Nokta Legend. This find was sold to a military museum for $4,500, and I shared the money 50/50 with the landowner. I'm incredibly proud that I finally found an old Revolutionary War item that will be displayed in a museum for everyone to appreciate.

53rd Regiment British Foot Soldier's Belt Plate

NATHAN DINNING

Bio: Nathan Dinning is from Merino, Victoria, Australia, and he hunts with a Minelab Equinox 900. He has enjoyed two metal detecting tours in England where he has recovered more than 150 coins, including six hammered and a Roman. The first coin he ever found was in the snow in England!

Find Info: Henry III Voided Long Cross Silver Hammered Penny (1248-50) which was recovered in Shropshire, England, in 2019. It is one of my favorite coins that I found as it reminds me of the incredible memories and the lifelong friendships that I made while metal detecting in England.

Henry III Voided Long Cross
1248-50

PAUL PRICE-TUPPER

Bio: Paul Price-Tupper is from Ashford, Kent, in the United Kingdom. He uses an XP Deus II and a Nokta Legend as a backup machine. Paul has around 1,400 hours on the Deus 2, documented in a log book kept. He is also known on YouTube and Instagram as "The Deeper Bleeper." Paul is a member of Invicta Seekers Metal Detecting Club.

Find Info: Found near Hamstreet, Kent, in April 2023, it is one of my favorite finds because it reminds me of pirate's treasure, as an 8 Real could be cut into 8 pieces and given back as change, hence the pirate saying 'pieces of eight.' It was also traded all around the world.

King Ferdinand II and Isabella I
1474-1504 Spanish 1 Real

PHIL MYERS

Bio: Phil Myers (aka Metal Detector Guru) is from Tampa, Florida. He has been metal detecting since the early 1980's and hunts with the Manticore, Deus 2 and Tarsacci MDT 8000. Phil is the owner of Myers Metal Detectors and one of the hosts for "Treasure Talk" live stream on YouTube and Facebook.

Find Info: One of my favorite finds is the US Belt Plate found in Tampa, formerly Fort Brooke, a Seminole War Fort Site established in 1824. The US belt plate is special to me, as I never thought I would find one in Tampa. I'm still searching for the gold coin, but as Mel Fisher said, "Today's the Day."

US Belt Plate
found in Tampa, Florida

ROB HILT

Bio: Rob Hilt is 51 years old and is from Wellsburg, West Virginia. He has been metal detecting for almost ten years and uses an XP Deus and a Minelab CTX 3030. Rob mainly detects in Washington County, which is located in Southwest Pennsylvania.

Find Info: This Shako Hat Plate came from a cabin site along what is now Route 844, and I worked with a local historical society to locate the home. This gentleman was a Colonel in the Washington County Militia, and the three homes he built for his daughters were all still standing, but his cabin site had not yet been found. Other items recovered from this long-lost cabin site included a solid silver knee buckle and an Eagle Anchor button.

Shako Hat Plate
Early 1800s

ROBERT JOHNSON

Bio: Robert Johnson is from New Jersey and has been metal detecting for more than 10 years. He hunts with the Garrett AT Pro, Garrett Infinium LS, and the Minelab Equinox 800. Rob served in the United States Navy from 1986 to 1990 and is an accomplished martial artist.

Find Info: This 1892-S Barber half dollar was struck at the mint in San Francisco, California. It was recovered in a Southern New Jersey park that was originally part of an old farm. I have detected in this park many times over the past several years and have also recovered coins from the early to mid-1700s.

Barber Half Dollar
1892-S

SID PERRY

Bio: Sid lives in Bromsgrove, a little sleepy town in the heart of Worcestershire, UK. He has been absolutely hooked on metal detecting for well over 15 years now. He loves making videos on the finds he's recovered in the fields and showing the true excitement we all get when we find a keeper. Sid also enjoys helping others to understand how to use their machines and get the most out of them. Plenty of fun, finds, and laughter on his YouTube channel @englandshistory.

Find Info: The coin shown is a King Henry III voided long cross silver penny, one of the many coins that Rob Copper and I found in our scattered hoard.

1247-72 King Henry III Voided Long Cross Silver Penny

STEF TANGUAY

Bio: Stef is an avid relic hunter from Hebron, CT, who searches for colonial and early American relics and coins. She shares many of these finds on her YouTube channel "Stef Digs." She currently swings a Minelab Manticore and serves as a Minelab Detexpert, an officially appointed Minelab brand ambassador.

Find Info: I found this 1800 Draped Bust half dime in a cornfield that saw a lot of activity between 1650 and 1850. After having detected the field dozens of times with few targets remaining, I was over the moon to dig up such an incredibly rare piece of American history.

Draped Bust Half Dime
1800

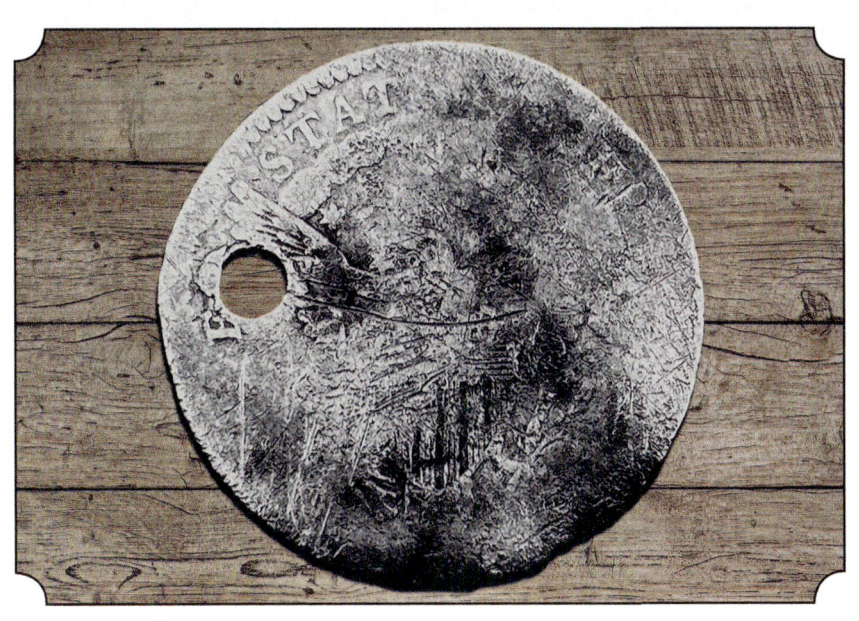

STEVE MOORE

Bio: Steve has been detecting since going to work for Garrett more than 17 years ago. He has detected in more than a dozen countries and 40 states. Steve enjoys participating in large organized hunts and rallies. Steve has authored more than two dozen non-fiction books on Texas history, World War II, Special Forces, and even metal detecting techniques.

Find Info: This was found during an organized hunt on an old plantation in Virginia. It was my first gold coin find, made with a Garrett AT Gold detector. My shovel didn't nick it, but it does have some damage that likely came from years of the field being plowed. But no matter, it's still a first I'll never forget. George 'KG' Wyant, who was hunting near me, spotted me taking photos of it. He tackled me to celebrate the find. The coin went flying, and I had to find it all over again! Funny but true.

Liberty Gold Dollar
1851

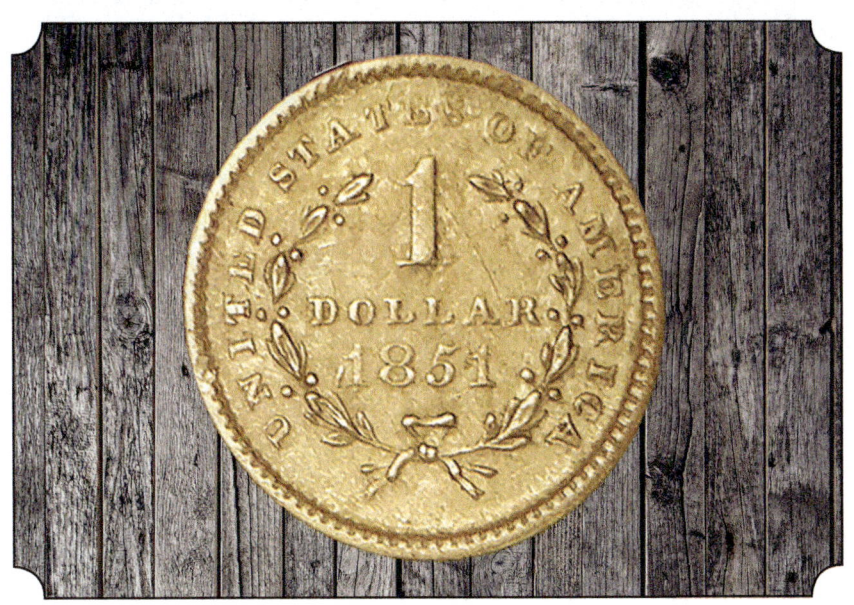

STEVE WARREN

Bio: Steve is a native Oklahoman and now lives in Palm Harbor, Florida. He swings a Minelab Equinox 800 and a Fisher F-75 LTD. Steve has pursued treasure and relics across the U.S. for 35 years. A journalist, TV producer, and Civil War historian, Steve is the author of "The Second Battle of Cabin Creek: Brilliant Victory" (The History Press: 2012) and the writer-producer of the documentary "Last Raid at Cabin Creek," which is available for streaming on Amazon Prime and Tubi. You can find Steve on social media @civilwarren. His motto is: "Keep Diggin' and Dream'n!"

Find Info: Used to remove obstructions from the vent hole of a cannon tube, this tool was dropped by Howell's Texas Battery during the Second Battle of Cabin Creek, Indian Territory, on September 19, 1864. I recovered it on the battlefield on November 25, 1994.

Confederate Artillery Gimlet
Second Battle of Cabin Creek

SUE ROBERTS

Bio: Sue lives in Richardson, Texas, and has been detecting since 2015. She hunts with the Garrett AT Pro, AT Max, and Troy Shadow X2. Sue also enjoys bottle digging, magnet fishing, and collecting old embossed bricks found during her adventures. She is the Secretary for the Lone Star Treasure Hunters Club and is a member of the Texas Association of Metal Detecting Clubs.

Find Info: This token for Jack & Pete's Place in Dallas was found with the Garrett AT-Max while hunting at an abandoned lot near Woodrow Wilson High School, near downtown Dallas. The school was built in 1928 and is still in use today.

Jack & Pete's Place Aluminium Token

TOM GEER

Bio: Tom lives in Central New York and has been metal detecting for many years. He hunts with the Minelab Equinox 800. Tom loves spending time researching and walking fields, trying to locate colonial and fur trade sites. He has a deep appreciation for the craftsmanship of the hardworking people who settled and started our great country.

Find Info: I recently unearthed this rare 1850-1860 New York Militia Civil War waist belt plate. The plate had sustained some damage from a farm implement, and fortunately, the belt loop was found a few feet away. I chose to have JP Relics repair the damage, and the results were fabulous!

New York Militia
Civil War Waist Belt Plate

117

TONY MANTIA

Bio: Tony (aka Bell-Two) has been detecting for more than 15 years and uses XP Deus I and Deus II detectors. He is a founding member and officer of the Dayton Diggers metal detecting club. Tony enjoys giving presentations to historical societies, schools, libraries, and other civic groups about metal detecting and the history they uncover.

Find Info: Army of Tennessee Confederate Belt Plate discovered in a bean field in Southwest Ohio! My research revealed that a resident from the home site was in the 90th OVI, which guarded 3,500 Confederate prisoners at Bridgeport, Alabama, providing a great opportunity to obtain this souvenir.

Army of Tennessee Confederate Belt Plate

Printed in Great Britain
by Amazon